WHEN
DISASTER
STRIKES
EXTREME
VOLCANOES

Thanks to the creative team:

Senior Editor: Alice Peebles
Fact checking: Tom Jackson
Illustration: Jeremy Pyke
Picture Research: Nic Dean
Design: www.collaborate.agency

First published in Great Britain in 2017
by Hungry Tomato Ltd
PO Box 181
Edenbridge
Kent, TN8 9DP

A CIP catalogue record for this book is
available from the British Library.

ISBN 978-1-912108-00-8

Printed and bound in China

Discover more at
www.hungrytomato.com

WHEN DISASTER STRIKES
EXTREME VOLCANOES

by John Farndon

HUNGRY
TOMATO.

CONTENTS

VOLCANOES

A volcano is a place on the Earth's surface where molten rock from its hot interior bursts through its solid crust. Sometimes, it is just a crack where the molten rock, known as magma, oozes through as lava (which is the name for magma on the surface). Sometimes, though, it is a cone-shaped mountain built up by successive eruptions. Mountain volcanoes can erupt in sudden and dramatic explosions, unleashing huge amounts of scorching hot material in one blast.

HOW DOES A VOLCANO HAPPEN?

Beneath most mountain volcanoes there is a reservoir of hot magma (molten rock) called the magma chamber. Over time, pressure builds up in the chamber as magma builds up from beneath. Eventually, the pressure is enough to drive the magma out on to the surface through the volcano's narrow chimney or 'vent'.

EYEWITNESS

Plinian eruptions are named after the terrible eruption of Vesuvius in Italy in 79 CE, which killed Roman scholar Pliny the Elder and was witnessed by his nephew from a boat at sea.

Lightning strikes caused by a build-up of static electricity are common in the most violent eruptions

The eruption blasts out fragments of the clog in the vent in a cloud of ash and debris

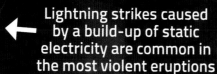

Large fragments called 'volcanic bombs' rain down around the mountain

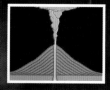

Sometimes, magma may burst through the side of the volcano to form smaller 'secondary cones'

Main vent

Once the ash and debris is blasted out of the way, molten magma floods out and runs down the mountain as streams of lava

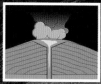

THERE SHE BLOWS!

In an explosive volcano, the vent is clogged up with solidified material from previous eruptions. A new eruption begins when rising magma pushes its way through the clog. As the magma bursts through, the pressure in it drops. Bubbles of carbon dioxide gas and steam suddenly form and drive the magma whooshing out like a fizzy drink from a shaken bottle.

The magma chamber, where magma builds up beneath the volcano before an eruption

KINDS OF ERUPTION

These are just some of the different kinds of volcanic eruption:

Plinian eruptions are the most violent, rocketing gas and volcanic ash high in the air, where they spread out far and wide in a flat-topped cloud.

Vulcanian eruptions produce less violent explosions of gas that are laden with volcanic ash and form dark, churning clouds. These billow quickly in convoluted shapes.

Strombolian eruptions occur in quick bursts, in which ash mixes with glowing globs of hot lava.

Pelean eruptions throw out high-speed avalanches of scorching hot ash and debris called pyroclastic flows.

Hawaiian eruptions are less violent but more continuous, emitting floods of runny lava that flow far out, cool and solidify to form shallow 'shield' volcanoes (see p. 10).

FAST AND FURIOUS

Super-explosive 'plinian' eruptions send out giant blast after giant blast of gas and volcanic ash, along with hot fragments of bubbly solidified lava called pumice. They rarely last more than a few weeks and sometimes less than a day.

BIG BANG

The explosive eruption of Mount Pinatubo, in the Philippines on 15 June 1991 was one of the biggest eruptions in recent history. It sent out high-speed avalanches of hot ash and gas (pyroclastic flows), giant mudflows (lahars) and a cloud of volcanic ash hundreds of miles across.

EXTREME VOLCANO DAMAGE

Volcanic eruptions can do terrible damage in many ways. They can send out suffocating clouds of gas and ash. They can bomb the surrounding area with red-hot fragments. They can belch unstoppable streams of red-hot lava, and scorching avalanches that destroy everything in their path. They can even set off earthquakes and landslides.

KINDS OF VOLCANO

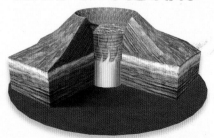

Caldera complexes have a 'caldera' (crater), from the mountain sinking into the magma chamber, like those in Yellowstone Park.

Dome volcanoes form from sticky lava glugging out into a dome-shaped mound. France's Puy de Dome is an extinct dome.

Fissure volcanoes are long cracks in the ground where lava oozes out continually with little explosive activity, as in Iceland.

Shield volcanoes form from runny lava flowing out far and wide. Hawaii's Mauna Kea is a shield volcano.

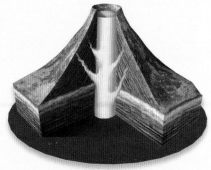

Stratovolcanoes or 'composites', such as Mount Etna in Sicily, are made of layers of lava and ash from successive eruptions.

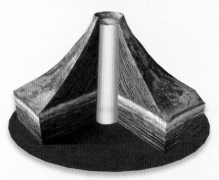

Ash and cinder cone volcanoes are cone-shaped mountains formed from ash and cinder. Krakatoa is a cinder cone.

MUDSLIDE

Some eruptions can set off devastating flows of scalding rock, mud and water called lahars. They typically start when the heat of an eruption melts snow or frozen ground. The mud hurtles downhill as fast as a car. When a lahar hit the city of Armero after the Nevado del Ruiz eruption in Colombia in 1985, 23,000 people were killed.

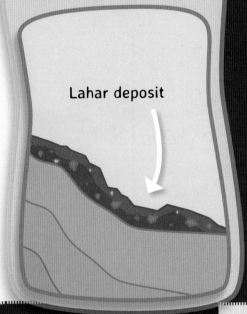

Lahar deposit

A VOLCANO'S ARMOURY

Volcanoes can throw up many kinds of danger!

• Lava flows — streams of red hot, molten rock — are terrifying and unstoppable, but usually move slowly enough for people to run away. But they destroy buildings.

• Scorching, choking clouds of ash and cinder falling far from the volcano are the big danger and there is little chance of escape. The weight of ash makes roofs collapse.

• Fine dust formed from volcanic debris can float gradually down and cause slow suffocation.

• Pyroclastic flows are superhot, high-speed avalanches of ash, cinders and gas.

GASSED!

In one of the eeriest volcanic disasters, more than 1,700 people and many animals were killed invisibly within minutes in Cameroon on 21 August 1986. The cause was a cloud of suffocating carbon dioxide gas released from nearby Lake Nyos. The lake was pumped full of the dangerous gas by mild volcanic eruptions from below the lake.

THE MOST DANGEROUS VOLCANOES

Getting caught near an erupting volcano is very dangerous. Yet many people live near volcanoes that have not erupted for so long they seem safe to live near. But are they really 'extinct' (stopped completely) or 'dormant' (sleeping) – or just biding their time until the next devastating eruption?

SHOCK ERUPTION

In 1980, most people thought Mount St. Helens in Washington was dead, since there had been no activity for over 100 years. But on 20 March that year, it suddenly exploded with the deadliest and costliest eruption in US history, killing 57 people.

ACTIVE VOLCANOES

There are no firm rules about what makes a volcano active, dormant or extinct. But when you can see smoke or lava pouring out, as in Kilauea in Hawaii, Sakurajima in Japan, or Cotopaxi (above) in Ecuador, you know it's active! Volcano scientists usually say that if it's erupted in the last 10,000 years, it's active.

DORMANT VOLCANOES

A dormant volcano is one that hasn't erupted for 10,000 years, yet still might erupt one day. Mount Kilimanjaro in Africa hasn't erupted for 360,000 years — but it's not entirely dead yet.

EXTINCT VOLCANOES

Extinct volcanoes have not erupted for tens or hundreds of thousands or even millions of years. They seem unlikely to erupt ever again because the magma beneath has gone cold and solid. Edinburgh Castle in Scotland is famously built on an extinct volcano.

ACTIVE OR SLEEPING?

Mount Fuji in Japan is one of the world's most famous volcanoes. It hasn't erupted for over 300 years. So is it sleeping, or is it preparing for a surprise? Small holes, called fumaroles, on the mountain release puffs of smoke even now. No one is sure if they are a danger sign or not.

SLEEPING GIANT

Mount Rainier in Washington looks calm and beautiful with its snowcapped peak. It hasn't erupted since 1894, so might seem to be sleeping. But a lot of people live nearby, and all that ice could melt in a terrible avalanche if it suddenly erupted.

EXTREME WEATHER EFFECTS

Volcanoes don't only make their impact felt on the ground and the landscape. They can change the atmosphere, too. When an explosive volcano erupts, it spews out so much ash and polluting gas into the atmosphere that this can actually change the weather not just locally, but right round the globe.

VOLCANIC STORM

As if you weren't frightened enough by all the debris and lava chucked out, a volcanic eruption often creates a violent storm, too! All the ash particles blasted high in the air attract water droplets. So the eruption becomes just like a super-intense thundercloud, with lots of rain, thunder and lightning flashes.

NASTY VOG

Eruptions in Hawaii are gentle, with lava oozing out continually. Yet these affect the weather. The lava tubes belch out fumes containing smelly sulphur dioxide. The gas combines with moisture over the sea to create a volcanic fog or 'vog' of sulphuric acid!

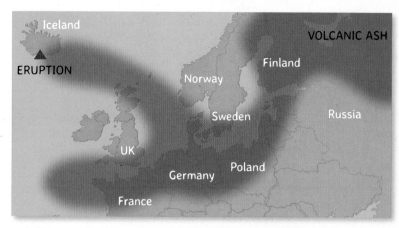

ASH MENACE

When Eyjafjallajökull volcano in Iceland erupted in 2010, it threw out a vast cloud of ash that was blown far over Western Europe. It was feared that the ash might have a catastrophic effect on the engines and electronics of jet planes. All planes were grounded for five days, and 95,000 flights were cancelled.

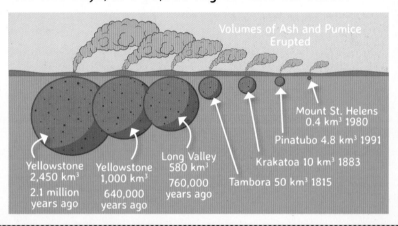

Volumes of Ash and Pumice Erupted

Yellowstone 2,450 km³ 2.1 million years ago

Yellowstone 1,000 km³ 640,000 years ago

Long Valley 580 km³ 760,000 years ago

Tambora 50 km³ 1815

Krakatoa 10 km³ 1883

Pinatubo 4.8 km³ 1991

Mount St. Helens 0.4 km³ 1980

A NARROW ESCAPE

On 24 June 1982, British Airways Flight 9 flew through ash from the eruption of Mount Galunggung in Indonesia. The captain calmly announced, 'All four engines have stopped. We are doing our damnedest to get them under control...' Fortunately, the engines restarted once the plane glided out of the ash cloud, and it landed safely!

EXTREME VOLCANOES IN HISTORY

Again and again throughout history, volcanoes have erupted and caused devastation. Many of the gigantic volcanic blasts have occurred in the 'Ring of Fire' around the Pacific Ocean, including Tambora (1815) and Krakatoa (1883). Meanwhile, people in Italy and Sicily have been faced with the dangers of volcanoes such as Vesuvius since ancient times.

UNBELIEVABLE!
There was a volcano located where the Greek island of Santorini is now. It erupted sometime between 1645 and 1500 BCE, in one of the biggest explosions ever witnessed.

TAMBORA 1815

The explosion of Mount Tambora on Sumbawa island, Indonesia, in April 1815 was the largest ever in recorded history. The noise was heard in Sumatra more than 1,930 km (1,200 miles) away. Around 71,000 people died, and ash clouds from the eruption spread worldwide and stopped summer coming to the northern hemisphere.

KRAKATOA 1883

Krakatoa is a volcanic island in the Sunda Strait in Indonesia. Its eruption on 26 August 1883 was one of the deadliest in recent history, killing nearly 40,000 people. It ejected huge amounts of rock, ash and pumice and was heard thousands of miles away. The explosion set off a tsunami, with waves up to 40 m (140 ft) high, that reached Arabia about 11,000 km (7,000 miles) away.

FIERY RING

Many of the world's most dangerous volcanoes form a 'Ring of Fire' around the Pacific Ocean, where tectonic plates — the giant slabs of rock that make up the Earth's crust — crunch together. Here, magma forces its way up through thick rock, making it super-sticky. Super-sticky magma frequently clogs up the volcanic vent so that pressure builds up until the clog bursts explosively.

Asia

Aleutian Trench

Mount St. Helens (Washington, USA)

North America

Mount Fuji (Japan)

RING OF FIRE

Parícutin (Mexico)

Mount Pinatubo (Philippines)

Mariana Trench

South America

Tonga Trench

Peru-Chile Trench

Australia

VESUVIUS 79

In 79 CE, Mount Vesuvius, near the modern city of Naples, erupted and buried the Roman towns of Pompeii and Herculaneum in rock and dust, killing thousands. The ashfall preserved much of the towns, as well as the body shapes of victims, as if in a time capsule. Some think Vesuvius is the most dangerous volcano today, since three million people live nearby.

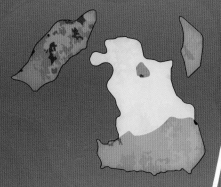

The island of Krakatoa was almost all destroyed in the 1883 eruption (right), but new eruptions beginning in December 1927 built the Anak Krakatau (Child of Krakatoa) in the same place.

I WAS THERE

Chances Peak is a volcano in the Soufrière Hills on the Caribbean island of Montserrat. Before 1995, it had been dormant for over 300 years. But that year it started to rumble and spew out dust and ash. By 1997, it was erupting continuously, setting off pyroclastic flows and lahars so devastating that people had to be evacuated.

PLYMOUTH DESTROYED

Montserrat's capital, Plymouth, was buried under layers of ash and mud. Many homes and buildings across the southern half of the island were lost, including the only hospital and the airport.

GETTING OUT

Evacuating all the island's people in time was a hazardous task, especially since the airport was destroyed. The British warship HMS *Liverpool* played a key role in taking people off the island. Some went to the neighbouring islands of Antigua and Barbuda. Many went all the way to the UK.

DOME VOLCANO

The lava from the Montserrat volcano is very sticky and cannot easily flow away from the vent. So instead it has piled up into a large, dome-shaped mass. The eruptions frequently blast solidified magma out as clouds of ash and pyroclastic flows.

SCORCHING FLOWS

The most dangerous features of the Montserrat eruptions were the pyroclastic flows: racing streams of scorching ash that incinerated everything in their path. People who stayed on to try and protect their homes believed they could guess when the flows were coming and make it to safety. Sadly, they were not always right.

WHY LIVE IN THE WAY?

Today, nearly half a billion people live on or close to active volcanoes. There are even major cities close to active volcanoes. For example, Mexico City is near Popocatapetl, and Naples near Vesuvius in Italy. They are dangerous places to live. But for the people who live there, the benefits outweigh the dangers.

IN THE VOLCANO'S CRADLE

In Kamchatka in the far east of Russia, 180,000 people live in the port city of Petropavlovsk-Kamchatsky — completely surrounded by active volcanoes. The volcanoes are dangerous though very beautiful, but the port gives access to the Pacific Ocean for ships and for fishing, making the risks worthwhile for the inhabitants.

INTO HELL

Miners work in the crater of East Java's Ijen volcano, collecting sulphur to make matches and fertilizer, and vulcanizing rubber for car tyres. Even if there is no eruption, the water in the crater is acidic enough to dissolve clothes, eat through metal and damage lungs!

THE WILDEBEEST NURSERY

Ol Doinyo Lengai means 'Mountain of God' in the language of the local Maasai people of Kenya. It is an active volcano that throws out a unique 'carbonatite' ash that makes the soil around the volcano very good for grass. The rich pastures are the reason that wildebeest stop here to give birth to calves on their long annual migration. The grasslands also attract Maasai herdsmen.

VINTAGE VOLCANO

Many wine growers say wine grown on volcanic soil is the best. Volcanic ash makes light, well-drained soil, rich in nutrients such as magnesium, calcium, sodium, iron and potassium. So Sicilian wine growers risk the dangers to grow grapes on the slopes of Mount Etna.

ONE STEP AHEAD OF THE VOLCANO

Volcano experts are called volcanologists, and it is their task to learn about volcanoes and detect signs ahead of an eruption to warn people living nearby. They look for clues such as pressure building up in the magma chamber beneath a volcano, or unusual gases being released. But monitoring a volcano can be a dangerous business.

UNBELIEVABLE!
A change in the chemistry of lava could warn of a coming eruption. So volcanologists wear protective clothing to take samples from a fresh, hot lava stream.

DRONES IN ACTION

Robot flying machines called drones are becoming important weapons in the volcanologist's armoury. They can fly right inside a volcano's crater where no human would dare set foot. Here, they may detect the clearest possible signs that a volcano is likely to erupt.

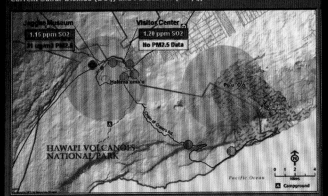

Hawai`i Volcanoes National Park
Current Sulfur Dioxide (SO₂) and Particulate (PM₂.₅) Conditions

The map above indicates the approximate direction and extent of the volcanic gas plumes (yellow wedges) from Halema'uma'u and Pu'u O'o. Within the plumes are unhealthy concentrations of sulfur dioxide (SO₂) and small particles (PM₂.₅). Color-coded health advisories (color circles or label boxes) are issued when the plumes affect surface areas.

...ulfur dioxide gas plumes cross roads near Halema`uma`u and low on ...ain of Craters Road. Sensitive individuals should limit exposure in these...

LOOKING FOR GAS

When a volcano is about to erupt, magma moves up the vent and begins to give off gases such as sulphur dioxide and hydrogen sulphide. If volcanologists can get close enough, they might be able to detect rises in these gases in the smoke billowing from side chimneys called fumaroles, or in the chemistry of crater lakes.

GROUND SHIFT

A telltale sign of magma pressure building up under a volcano could be a slight change in the volcano's shape. Meters are placed in the ground on a volcano and with the aid of GPS satellites they can detect changes of just a few millimetres in the shape of the ground. Even a small change like this might indicate an imminent eruption.

GROUND SHAKING

For many volcanologists, the key clue to a coming eruption is 'seismic activity'. By this they mean the ground on the volcano shaking and rumbling a little. Almost all the world's major volcanoes are now continually monitored for any shaking, using seismometers either slightly away from the volcano or right on its slopes.

COMPARING ERUPTIONS

Volcanologists compare the scale of eruptions using the Volcanic Explosive Index (VEI). It uses things such as volume of ash and cloud height to indicate just how explosive an eruption was, from gentle (0) to mega-colossal (8).

UNSEEN EXTREME VOLCANOES

Many volcanoes, like Fujiyama or Kilimanjaro, are hard to miss, towering high above their surroundings. But many others are almost entirely invisible, erupting out of sight under the sea. Indeed, there are thought to be a million or more volcanoes below sea level, producing more than three-quarters of all the magma erupted on Earth.

EYEWITNESS

On 14 November 1963, crew of the fishing boat Ísleifur II spotted dark smoke over the sea south of Iceland. It was not a boat on fire, as they thought, but the new island of Surtsey being born. In a few days, it had reached over 500 m (1,640 ft) long and 45 m (147 ft) high.

The Mid-Atlantic Ridge can be seen briefly above the sea in Iceland's Thingvellir gorge.

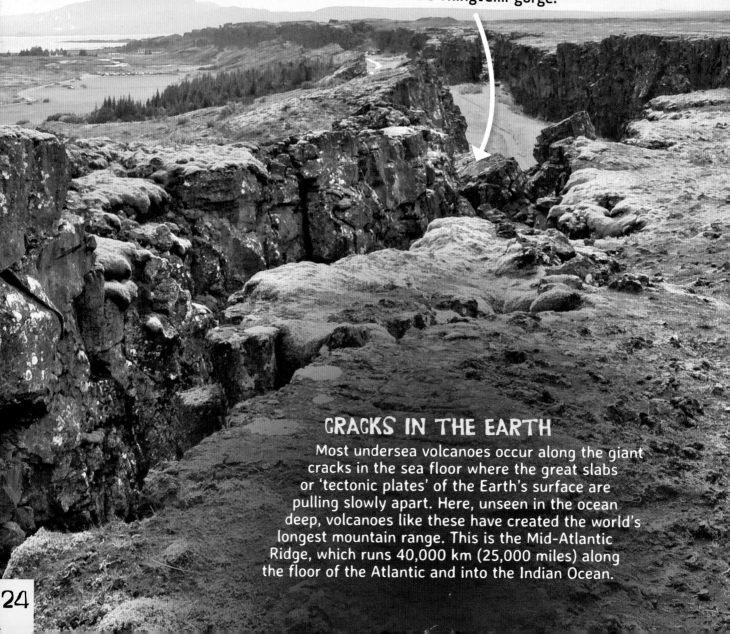

CRACKS IN THE EARTH

Most undersea volcanoes occur along the giant cracks in the sea floor where the great slabs or 'tectonic plates' of the Earth's surface are pulling slowly apart. Here, unseen in the ocean deep, volcanoes like these have created the world's longest mountain range. This is the Mid-Atlantic Ridge, which runs 40,000 km (25,000 miles) along the floor of the Atlantic and into the Indian Ocean.

BLACK SMOKERS

Geysers like Yellowstone's Old Faithful are chimneys where bursts of superhot water whoosh out after it is heated under pressure by volcanic activity underground. Amazingly, there are geysers, or 'hydrothermal vents', under the sea, too. Only they are called 'black smokers' because the jets of water are mixed in with dark clouds of minerals.

Black smoker

Water seeping through ocean floor

Super-heated water

Heat from magma below

HOT GIANT

Hawaii's Mauna Kea is 10,000 m (32,800 ft) tall, taller than Everest's 8,850 m (29,035 ft)! But most of it is underwater. Mauna Kea is a 'hot spot' volcano. 'Hot spots' are rare places where fountains of hot molten rock rise up through the Earth's interior and scorch their way out through the crust.

NEW ISLANDS

New islands can appear in the sea overnight, when an undersea volcano grows high enough to erupt above the surface. This happened at Hunga Tonga in the Pacific in 2009, Nishinoshima in Japan in 1973 and, even more spectacularly, with the island of Surtsey off Iceland in 1963.

EXTREME ERUPTIONS

Every now and then in Earth's history, there have been volcanic events so mighty that they have created worldwide cataclysms. Some 252 million years ago, 96% of all sea creatures and 70% of all land creatures may have been wiped out when volcanic eruptions poisoned the air and caused massive global warming. Could such a terrible event happen again?

THE WORLD'S GREATEST DISASTER

Scientists call the terrible event that wiped out so much life on Earth the 'Permian-Triassic Mass Extinction', or more simply the 'Great Dying'. Some think the damage was done by a giant meteorite smashing into the Earth. But most think it was triggered by a continuous series of massive eruptions in Siberia. These spread 2,000,000 km² (770,000 square miles) of lava over Siberia, called the Siberian Traps. The eruptions also released gases and ash that turned rain acid and trapped so much of the sun's heat in the atmosphere that the world scorched.

COULD IT HAPPEN AGAIN?

It is certain that there will be a cataclysmic 'supervolcano' eruption like Yellowstone (below) in the future. And there is no way to prevent it. But scientists are trying to discover ways of monitoring the pressure of underground magma to predict whether one is imminent. Most experts agree that no supervolcano is likely to erupt in the foreseeable future. But the foreseeable future spans just 10 years...

HUMAN ESCAPE?

Around 75,000 years ago, one of the largest ever volcanic eruptions, of Toba in Indonesia, flung huge amounts of ash and dust into the air. As all this material spread around the world, it blocked out the sun and made the world turn icy cold. It's thought that only a handful of humans — just a few thousand — made it through this terrible time. That may be why today we all have the same few ancestors from back then.

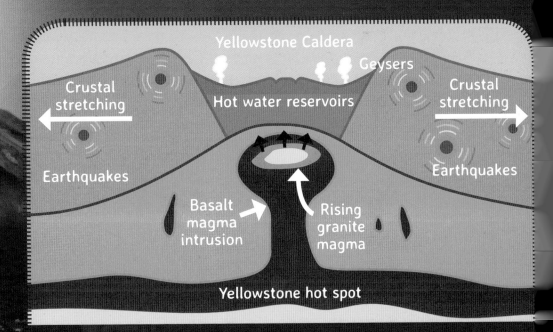

Yellowstone Caldera

Geysers

Crustal stretching

Hot water reservoirs

Crustal stretching

Earthquakes

Earthquakes

Basalt magma intrusion

Rising granite magma

Yellowstone hot spot

YELLOWSTONE SUPERVOLCANO

Yellowstone is actually one of the world's biggest volcanoes. It is what volcanologists call a 'supervolcano'. It last erupted 640,000 years ago, flooding the region with enough lava to fill up the Grand Canyon. Yellowstone looks fairly mild today, but it is now overdue for another eruption. Scientists think that if it did erupt, the USA would be covered in ash more than 1 m (3 ft) deep.

...ELINE

1645-1500 BCE
The island volcano of Thera in the Mediterranean erupted in the largest explosion ever witnessed by humans

79 CE
The eruption of Mount Vesuvius in Italy smothered the Roman towns of Pompeii and Herculaneum in thick ash

1600
The biggest eruption in American history, of Huaynaputina in Peru, destroyed the city of Arequipa and created a cloud of ash that affected weather worldwide and caused a famine in Russia

1815
The eruption of Tambora in Indonesia was the biggest in recent history. The vast amounts of ash thrown up caused a cool summer around the world

...ion years ago
...ve lava eruption in ...now southern India ...the Deccan Traps, a ...va plateau twice the ...Texas

27,000 years ago
A supervolcano eruption on North Island, New Zealand, created the enormous crater now filled by Lake Taupo

1883
Krakatoa in the Sunda Strait, Indonesia, erupted with a bang heard thousands of miles away and triggered a massive tsunami

640,000 years ago
A supervolcano erupted (again) to create the Yellowstone area

1783
The eruption of Laki in Iceland spread poisonous gases across Western Europe

...on years ago
...on Island
...tlantic was
...by a volcanic
...n

1902
On the French island of Martinique in the Caribbean, a pyroclastic flow from the eruption of Mount Pelée killed over 29,000 people in the town of St. Pierre

1980
Mount St. Helens in Washington state erupted with the most devastating eruption in US history, killing 57 people and doing huge damage

1963
The Icelandic island of Surtsey was created by an undersea volcanic eruption

1985
A mudslide triggered by the eruption of Colombia's Nevado del Ruiz volcano killed 23,000 people

1991
The eruption of Pinatubo in the Philippines ejected more than 4 km³ (1 cubic mile) of material into the air and sent up a column of ash 35 km (22 miles) high

2011

1982
El Chichón began to erupt in Mexico

2010
Dust from the eruption of Eyjafjallajökull in Iceland downed all air flights in Western Europe.

Mount Merapi in Java erupted, forcing the evacuation of 350,000 people

1983
Kilauea began to erupt in Hawaii

1912
Novarupta in Alaska was the biggest eruption of the 20th century and drained magma from nearby Mount Katmai, making it collapse

1986
A cloud of carbon dioxide bubbling from under Lake Nyos in Cameroon suffocated 1,746 people

EXPLOSIVE

Amazing facts about volcanoes

There are some big volcanoes on Earth, but the biggest in the solar system is on Mars. Its name is Olympus Mons and it is gigantic: 600 km (373 miles) wide and 21 km (13 miles) high.

HIGH PEAK

The furthest point from the centre of the Earth is not the peak of Mount Everest, but the peak of the volcano Chimborazo in Ecuador. This is because the Earth spins very fast and so it bulges in the middle. This makes it fatter at the equator, and Chimborazo is very near the equator.

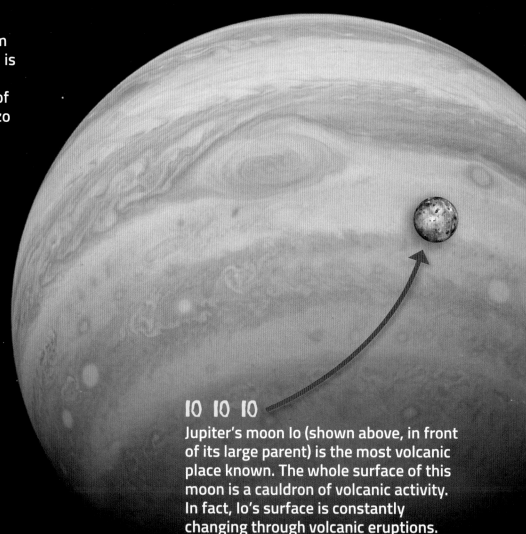

IO IO IO

Jupiter's moon Io (shown above, in front of its large parent) is the most volcanic place known. The whole surface of this moon is a cauldron of volcanic activity. In fact, Io's surface is constantly changing through volcanic eruptions.

LIGHT ROCK

Pumice is a very light and porous rock that forms when the glassy froth of lava cools and solidifies. It is the rock that actually floats!

HAPPENING NOW

There are at least 20 volcanoes erupting around the world at this very moment! Between 50 and 70 volcanoes erupt every year, and over the last decade about 160 have been active. Scientist estimate that in the last 10,000 years, 1,300 volcanoes erupted.

VOLCANIC HATCHERY

On the Indonesian island of Sulawesi, maleo birds don't sit on their eggs to keep them warm. They cleverly use volcanic heat to help hatch their eggs! They bury the eggs in soil or sand near volcanoes. When the chicks hatch, they claw their way up to the surface.

HOT LAVA

Lava might not always move very fast, but you don't want to stand in its way. Its temperature can reach 1,250° C (2,280° F) and will burn through pretty much everything!

VOLCANIC WORLD

We owe much of our world to volcanoes. More than 80 per cent of Earth's crust was made by volcanoes. Although a lot is now covered with a veneer of sediments, most sediments are fragments of crumbled volcanic rock. The sea floor and some mountains were formed by countless volcanic eruptions. Gases from volcanoes also formed Earth's atmosphere.

WORST VOLCANIC ERUPTIONS

LARGEST ERUPTION EVER

Guarapuava-Tamarana-Sarusas, Paraná Traps, Brazil
132 million years ago (mya)
Volume: 8,600 km³ (2,000 cubic miles)
— enough to cover New York state to a depth of over 60 m (195 ft)

LARGEST IN THE LAST 25 MILLION YEARS

Lake Toba, Sunda Arc, Indonesia
75,000 years ago
Volume: 2,800 km³ (670 cubic miles)
— enough to cover New York state to a depth of over 20 m (65 ft)

LARGEST IN THE LAST 50,000 YEARS

Taupo, New Zealand
27,000 years ago
Volume: 1,170 km³ (280 cubic miles)

LARGEST ERUPTION OF LAVA

Mahabaleshwar-Rajahmundry Traps, Deccan Traps, India
65 mya
Volume: 9,300 km³ (2,200 cubic miles)
— enough to cover New York state to a depth of over 70 m (230 ft)

LARGEST VOLCANIC ACCUMULATION

Ontong Java-Manihiki-Hikurangi Plateau, southwest Pacific Ocean
121 mya
Volume: 67,000,000 km³ (16,000,000 cubic miles) — enough to cover the whole of the USA to a depth of almost 7 km (4 miles)

DEADLIEST ERUPTION

Mount Tambora, Indonesia, 1815
Cost in lives: 92,000

DEADLIEST IN THE LAST CENTURY

Mount Pelée, Martinique, 1902
Cost in lives: 29,025

DEADLIEST IN THE LAST 50 YEARS

Mount Pinatubo, Philippines, 1991
Cost in lives: 800

DEADLIEST VOLCANIC EFFECTS

Huaynaputina, Peru, 1600
Cost in lives: 2 million Russians died of famine after the huge ash cloud caused extremely cold weather across the world

INDEX

THE AUTHOR

John Farndon is Royal Literary Fellow at City&Guilds in London, UK, and the author of a huge number of books for adults and children on science, technology and nature, including such international best-sellers as *Do Not Open* and *Do You Think You're Clever?* He has been shortlisted six times for the Royal Society's Young People's Book Prize for a science book, with titles such as *How the Earth Works, What Happens When?* and *Project Body* (2016).